# STUCK!
## Seven Questions to Conquer Spiritual Stagnation

Larry Dixon, Ph.D

Energion Publications
Cantonment, Florida
2025

Original cartoons by . . .
Ron Wheeler
Ron.Wheeler@Navigators.org
ron@cartoonworks.com

ISBN: 978-1-63199-923-9
eISBN: 978-1-63199-924-6


Energion Publications
1241 Conference Rd
Cantonment, FL 32533

energion.com
pubs@energion.com

# Table of Contents

# INTRODUCTION

I've never been caught up in quicksand. I've been plenty muddy, especially when I was a little kid. And I had some really great adventures in my sandbox which my mother sold on Ebay when I was 18. I'm still working on my bitterness.

Now that I think about it — why don't we set up **quick**sand-boxes for our children and grandchildren? They don't have to be 8 feet deep or anything. That would be dangerous. But a few inches would teach them that life sometimes sucks you down and all you can do is cry, "Mommmmmy!"

Quicksand is an apt metaphor for getting stuck in the Christian life. One car commercial asks, "Why is it called 'quicksand' when it works slow? Shouldn't it be called 'slowsand'?"

Whatever we choose to call it, spiritual stuckness is real, progressive, and lethal. This book attempts to offer a biblical branch or two to grab onto if you see yourself stuck and sinking.

## A Few Questions

How would you describe your spiritual life right now? Not when you're sitting in church or having lunch with your pastor or doing your duty in Vacation Bible School. I mean right now as you read this.

If your answer is: "I'm just fine. Thank you. I'm progressing nicely in my walk with Jesus. I certainly wouldn't describe my life as 'stuck.' And I'm kind of upset that you would even suggest that I'm 'stuck'!" Then this book is probably not for you. Go get your money back. (You might want to work on your bitterness too. Just saying).

If, however, you find yourself a bit discouraged with your progress in the Christian life, if you would appreciate some direct questions to help you assess where you might need to focus some attention, if you're open to being challenged with some practical and specific truths, this book might just help.

Here's a brief summary of what each of these seven chapters will discuss.

## Chapter 1- WHO'S IN CHARGE?

If you had to lay blame on someone for your lack of spiritual progress, who would you blame? Your pastor? Your spouse? Your children? A televangelist or two? Or would you say, "I won't play the blame game. I'm responsible for where I am right now."

I was reading through Proverbs 1 the other day and came across a fascinating statement about the wicked in verse 18. There we read, "These men lie in wait for their own blood; *they ambush only themselves!*" I think the idea of a self-ambush is quite appropriate for the times I've gotten stuck.[1]

## Chapter 2- WHO SEZ?

How critical is the Bible in your life right now? Would you describe your Bible as only a kind of clothing accessory for your Sunday dress for church? Do you see the Word of God as a magic book or maybe as a simple collection of really wise proverbs for those struggling with rebellious teenagers or irritating neighbors? What practical use do you make of the Bible?

## Chapter 3- WHY SHOULD I CARE?

How do you view other people? I'm an introvert so I can pretty well do without people. How do you look at total  strangers, the

---

1   There's another, more in-your-face, metaphor found in James 1:13-15 regarding the issue of temptation. And I can't think of a better way to describe that metaphor than self-rape!

young guy who gets your caramel latte at Starbucks, the plumber who's trying to unclog your toilet? Does the question "I wonder where they stand with Christ?" ever enter your mind?

## Chapter 4- WHO SHOULD I IMPACT?

"No man lives to himself and no man dies to himself," the Good Book says. We influence, affect, impact others. We're talking about the issue of discipleship. Who is helping you in your walk with the Lord? Into whose life are you pouring your own? This chapter discusses three areas of discipleship which we will call "Paul," "Barnabas," and "Timothy." I'll bet you never thought of naming a level of discipleship, right?

## Chapter 5- WHO DO I NEED?

I'm sure you've seen the sign in front of the church that reads: "CH__CH! What's missing? Answer: U R!" For many genuinely born-again believers the local church is the great option. All they need is a pandemic to force them to stay home in their pajamas and not return to the church. Oh, wait! That's just happened! But who really needs the local church? And why?

## Chapter 6- WHERE DO I START?

For those who feel they are somewhat stuck in their spiritual lives, I've got great news! Change is possible! Choices can be made which will radically alter your present life! Really. We will discuss what are called "the spiritual disciplines" or, as I would prefer to call them, "the holy habits."

["Disciplines" sounds like I've been called in to the principle's office. Again].

# Chapter 7- HOW DOES THIS END?

Spiritual growth in the Christian life will one day reach both an end and a beginning. The end will be when each of us dies and we no longer can make choices to grow in godliness. If I understand my Bible, the Lord then takes over and completes the sanctification process, finishing the task of making us like the Lord Jesus (what theologians call "glorification"). In a sense, that will be the end of our earthly spiritual growth process. But that moment will also initiate an incredible beginning of worshiping, praising, and serving the Lord in resurrection bodies without sin! A new creation! But there will be a judgment for the people of God — and we must think about that judgment before it happens.

## In Conclusion

A short article entitled "Self Soul-Care: A Challenge for Self-Directed Learning" completes our study. The implications of Jesus' invitation in Matthew 11 ("Come to me, all you who are weary and burdened, and I will give you rest. Take my yoke upon you and learn from me, for I am gentle and humble in heart, and you will find rest for your souls. For my yoke is easy and my burden is light.") are examined and applied.

# CHAPTER ONE:

# WHO'S IN CHARGE?

"Quicksand is a shear thinning non-Newtonian fluid: when undisturbed, it often appears to be solid ('gel' form), but a less than 1% change in the stress on the quicksand will cause a sudden decrease in its viscosity ('sol' form). After an initial disturbance—such as a person attempting to walk on it—the water and sand in the quicksand separate and dense regions of sand sediment form; it is because of the formation of these high volume fraction regions that the viscosity of the quicksand seems to decrease suddenly. Someone stepping on it will start to sink."[1]

"So there you have it: Nature is a rotten mess. But that's only the beginning. If you take your eyes off it for one second, it will kill you. Thorns, insects, fungus, worms, birds, reptiles, wild animals, raging rivers, bottomless ravines, dry deserts, snow, quicksand, tumbleweeds, sap, and mud. Rot, poison

1   https://en.wikipedia.org/wiki/Quicksand.

and death. That's Nature. It's a wonder you even step outside of your cabin, I said. My bravery exceeds my good sense, he said." ~ Lee Goldberg

Henry Wadsworth Longfellow once said, "Life hath quicksands, Life hath snares!"

> Getting unstuck begins with a simple acknowledgement: I am responsible for my walk with Jesus.

My questions would be: How did you get into the quicksand? Did somebody push you? Or did you simply wander in? Who's going to get you out?

There may or may not have been a warning sign that said, "Beware! Quicksand Ahead!" Getting stuck in the Christian life may not be intentional, but getting unstuck begins with a simple acknowledgement: I am responsible for my walk with Jesus. And I will give an account for how I lived it (a truth we will unpack in Chapter 7's "How Does This End?").

In this first chapter we want to emphasize the issue of personal responsibility. Who's in charge of your life? Now, the spiritual answer, of course, should be "Jesus." But we both know that that's only sometimes true.

There may be splotches of spirituality in your life once in a while, but the bottom line is that you control your daily activities. You decide what to think about. You choose what words to use and when to use them. You have the power to live your life 24/7 without recognizing that it is the Lord who gives you your very next lungful of air to breathe. And He gives you freedom to make wise or not so wise choices.

> We are saved by faith alone, but become like Christ by our faith *and* our works.

It's a long quote from C.S. Lewis, but well worth thinking about. Concerning our choices, Lewis writes —

Every time you make a choice you are turning the central part of you, the part of you that chooses, into something a little different than it was before. And taking your life as a whole, with all your innumerable choices, all your life long you are slowly turning this central thing into a heavenly creature or a hellish creature: either into a creature that is in harmony with God, and with other creatures, and with itself, or else into one that is in a state of war and hatred with God, and with its fellow creatures, and with itself. To be the one kind of creature is heaven: that is, it is joy and peace and knowledge and power. To be the other means madness, horror, idiocy, rage, impotence, and eternal loneliness. Each of us at each moment is progressing to the one state or the other. [2]

## The "Let Go and Let God" Myth

In the 19th and 20th centuries there was a movement sometimes referred to as the "Victorious Christian Life" movement. Also called the Keswick Movement, its basic message seemed to be a kind of passive Christian living which stressed God's work in making us like Christ. That's all well and good, but what about personal responsibility?

This movement said that not only are we saved by faith alone — but we are also sanctified by faith alone. Sanctification is a theologian's big word that means "set apart," "made holy." Pastor Kevin DeYoung writes,

> . . . we should not be afraid to talk about justification in a different way than we talk about sanctification. One calls us to rest; the other to fight. One *reckons* us righteous; the other *makes* us righteous. One allows for no increase or degrees; the

---

2  *Mere Christianity*, C. S. Lewis, Book III, Chapter 4, "Morality and Psychoanalysis", 1952. I appreciate the quote by Richelle E. Goodrich who said, "Some decisions in life naturally lead to an unhappy ending, leaving you sinking by degrees in a lake of quicksand. And, unless someone reaches to pull you out, chances are you will drown in the consequences."

other expects progress and growth. One is a declaration of God *about* us, the other a work of God *in* us. [3]

He helpfully writes further,

In sanctification, we don't just fight to believe (though every-thing flows from faith). We actually will and do. We don't just dive deeper into our justification, we perform a duty. We must be diligent to stir up the grace of God that is in us. This sort of language—willing, doing, perform[ing], diligence—has no place in talking about justification. But if we do not use this language in talking about sanctification we have missed the language of the Bible.[4]

It is more biblical to say that, yes, we are saved by faith alone, but we become like Christ by our faith — *and* our works.

We're all familiar with the famous passage in Ephesians 2, a text we often use with our unsaved friends. There we read —

8 For it is by grace you have been saved, through faith—and this is not from yourselves, it is the gift of God— 9 not by works, so that no one can boast.

We do our best to make it clear to our lost friends that they can't earn salvation by their good works. Trying to purchase the gift of God is insulting — and fruitless.

But we need to keep reading. The next verse gives the flip side of verses 8-9. There we read —

10 For we are God's handiwork, created in Christ Jesus to do good works, which God prepared in advance for us to do.

We can't be saved by our good works. But there's a world of good works to get cracking on after conversion![5] And those "good

3   https://www.thegospelcoalition.org/blogs/kevin-deyoung/is-sanctifica-tion-by-faith-alone/

4   Ibid.

5   The author Jessica Hagy once wrote, "An easy life is like quicksand: Before you know it, you're trapped and can't move, can't breathe, can't get to where you really wanted to go. Don't coast unless you're rolling downhill on a bicycle."

works" of verse 10 are not just external good deeds or philanthropic gestures. We are to get busy working on *ourselves*.

## The "Get Up! And Get Going!" Truth

What impression do we get from the Scriptures about growing in the Christian life? As I read my Bible I'm challenged to roll up my spiritual sleeves and get to work! The Apostle Peter makes it quite clear that, after one is saved, our works kick into high gear. We read in 2 Peter 1 —

> 5 For this very reason, make every effort to add to your faith goodness; and to goodness, knowledge; 6 and to knowledge, self-control; and to self-control, perseverance; and to persever-ance, godliness; 7 and to godliness, mutual affection; and to mutual affection, love. 8 For if you possess these qualities in increasing measure, they will keep you from being ineffective and unproductive in your knowledge of our Lord Jesus Christ. 9 But whoever does not have them is nearsighted and blind, forgetting that they have been cleansed from their past sins.

The idea here is that the believer is to hurry up and add to his faith. We are to "make every effort." The term "effort" is used of the girl that Herodias sent to Herod to ask for the head of John the Baptist on a platter ("at *once* the girl hurried in to the king", Mark 6:25). The term is also translated "eagerness" in 2 Corinthians 7:11 (see also Jude 1:3) and "earnestness" in Hebrews 6:11.

There should be no hesitation for the believer to get busy with great eagerness and serious earnestness to begin adding these virtues to his faith. The two verbs that follow this word "effort" indicate that we are to "bring in beside," to "superadd" these virtues to our faith. These verbs are not passive (indicating a waiting on God to produce these qualities), but active, emphasizing our responsibility to get going and get growing.

## God's Mathematics

The Christian life involves both *subtraction* (getting rid of our unholy habits) and *addition* (adding qualities to our lives that honor God). We are also to engage in *multiplication* (making disciples) and *division* (separating ourselves from evil and false doctrine). In this text Peter is hammering away at the addition-side of the Christian life.[6]

> The Christian life involves subtraction, addition, division, and multiplication.

He gives us a list of these seven hard-to-achieve godly qualities (goodness, knowledge, self-control, perseverance, godliness, mutual affection, love) which we are to add. These qualities won't be given to us as Christmas presents, awarded to us for faithful church attendance, or bequeathed us when a spiritual family member dies. WE are to ADD these qualities to our lives! The question is: Are you making "every effort" in adding these necessary components of the Christian life to your daily walk?

## Virtuous and Grievous Conclusions

Please notice several hard-hitting conclusions to which Peter comes in this passage. The *first* conclusion concerns the one who is following Peter's command and is adding to his faith: Adding these virtues will keep one from being ineffective or unproductive in your knowledge of Jesus Christ (v. 8). "Ineffective" is a word that can mean lazy or useless. Homer uses this term in his *Iliad* to mean "shunning the labor which one ought to perform." "Unproductive" carries the idea of being unfruitful. Growing in these

---

6   We get other texts that focus on the *subtracting* side of sanctification, such as "Get rid of all bitterness, rage and anger, brawling and slander, along with every form of malice." (Ephesians 4:31). Note also James 1:21 which says, "Therefore, get rid of all moral filth and the evil that is so prevalent and humbly accept the word planted in you, which can save you."

virtues is work. And God expects us to be fruitful. We are to labor to produce these qualities in our lives, not think and act as if we can simply glide to glory.

Please don't miss the point that one is to possess these qualities "in increasing measure." (v. 8) We don't get a one-and-done dose of self-control or perseverance or love when we roll up our sleeves and take responsibility. No. These qualities are to increase.

The *second* conclusion Peter makes relates to the one who doesn't have these qualities and, presumably, shows no interest in working toward them. The one who doesn't have these qualities has become blind and forgetful. Peter states that such a person "is nearsighted and blind" (v. 9). One who is near-sighted sees only what is in front of them. They have no vision of that which is distant or far off. He or she can't see what lies ahead. They see only what's close to them. It's bad to be near-sighted.

It's worse to be "blind." That's quite a charge Peter makes here in verse 9. The one not working on these virtues is not just near-sighted, but blind. Blind to what God wants to do in and through his life, blind to the sins that need to be shed, the temptations that need to be avoided, the opportunities which need to be taken advantage of.

I'm 75 and I sometimes forget things. Forgetfulness comes with old age. This person who is not actively seeking to add these virtues to his faith is like an aging man who is constantly forgetting. What exactly is this one who's not making the effort forgetting? *They are forgetting that they have been forgiven!* Can there be a worst thing to forget? Not working at adding these virtues to one's faith means the atoning

> Not to add the virtues of 2 Peter 1 to my life means the work of Christ is suitable only for forgetting.

work of Christ was worthless, ineffective, of no lasting value, and suitable only for forgetting.

There are many other passages that challenge the believer to take responsibility for his spiritual life, to get going, to turn away from spiritual stagnation. For example, we read in Jeremiah 6:16, "Thus saith the Lord, 'Stand ye in the ways, and see, and ask for the old paths, where is the good way, and walk therein, and ye shall find rest for your souls.' But they said, 'We will not walk therein.'" (KJV). Enoch walked with God, we read in Genesis 5:24. He didn't just stand around. And one day God essentially said to Enoch, "Enoch, we're closer to my house than to yours. Why don't you just come home with me?"

We are talking about the issue of sanctification, of course. If we find ourselves "stuck," God provides steps that we can take to move on in the Christian life, to really begin to walk with the Lord, to advance in godliness. But to do so involves asking and answering the most foundational question in our study and we will do so in our next chapter.

## Homework

1. In what ways do we sometimes seem to support a passive-kind of Christian life?
2. Of the seven virtues in 2 Peter 1, which one would you tackle first if you committed yourself to a serious pursuit of this kind of sanctified addition? Are you bold enough to ask someone who loves you which virtue *they* think you might need to work on?
3. Perhaps, like me, you need to pray a prayer of confession which might go something like this:

"Dear Lord, I confess that I have been way too passive about my Christian progress. Please forgive my laziness or lack of discipline or _____ (fill in the blank). Help me not to blame others for my getting stuck. Lord, give me specific steps to take to become more like the Lord Jesus. And help me to begin taking those steps right now. In Jesus' name. Amen."

# Chapter Two:

# Who Sez?

"Continued or panicked movement, however, may cause a person to sink further in the quicksand. Since this increasingly impairs movement, it can lead to a situation where other factors such as weather exposure (i.e. sun stroke), dehydration, hypothermia, drowning in a rising tide or predatory animals may harm a trapped person."[1]

"While theoretically a person may block God out, logically there will be a breakdown because ultimately all enunciation implies a moral doctrine of some kind. And if that moral doctrine is not absolute then the definer himself becomes undefined. That's what we are living with – an undefined definer giving us definitions for our course, and we are being trapped in the quicksand of the absence of objective truth." ~ Ravi Zacharias

---

1   https://brokendoorministries.com/4th-day-letters/quicksand/.

How are you going to get out of the quicksand you've stumbled into? Will you panic and try to follow your own best advice? Or listen to experts who know quicksand and how to escape it? We need authoritative advice about how to extricate ourselves from our spiritual quicksand.

In this chapter we want to deal with what is perhaps the most foundational question one can answer. The question is, "What is the authority for your life?" To ask the question another way, "Where do you get your beliefs, your priorities, the truth?" Francis Bacon, the English philosopher and statesman, once said, "People prefer to believe what they prefer to be true."[2]

> "People prefer to believe what they prefer to be true." (Francis Bacon)

If my authority is my own opinion, or the beliefs of my friends, or what the majority thinks or feels, my spiritual life is in a lot of trouble. My preferences have nothing to do with truth. My opinions are always changing, my friends don't seem to have a clue what they believe most of the time, and the majority is so frequently wrong! I need an unchanging, reliable, trustworthy source for my total life. And that should be the Word of God, the Bible.

## A Spiritual Accessory?

And here is the problem for a lot of Christians. For many they see God's Word as part of their Sunday go-to-meeting outfit, a necessary accessory to their ensemble. They carry a big Bible, preferably black, under their arm as they attend church. Or, for perhaps the majority today, it's simply an app on their phone which they can pull up to follow the preacher (or check their email when the sermon drags).

---

2   https://www.goodreads.com/quotes/63465-man-prefers-to-believe-what-he-prefers-to-be-true.

## The True Nature of God's Word

But in our heart of hearts we know the Bible is much more than a good luck charm (like a religious rabbit's foot). And reading the Bible should be much more than checking what amounts to some to be a daily holy horoscope. We need to see the Bible for what it truly is: God's instruction book for the believer. It tells us how to live, what to avoid, how to think, where to spend our time, what our mission is, how to deal with temptation and sin, when to engage others with the gospel (and when to walk away),[3] why there is suffering and sometimes why this (whatever catastrophe I'm going through at the moment) is happening to me now, etc.

> God's Word as a hidden treasure.

My wife and I have a small, online Amazon book business. We ship out about ten books a day. These are books we get at thrift stores, yard sales, etc. Every thrift store for us is a treasure hunt. You know, thinking rightly about the Word of God begins with understanding His truth as *a hidden treasure*. The Psalmist writes, "The law from your mouth is more precious to me than thousands of pieces of silver and gold." (Psalm 119:72).

Roger Miklos, one of the world's foremost modern day treasure hunters for a large salvage company, once said in 1978, "A very conservative estimate of the treasure still lost off the U.S. coast between North Carolina and Florida [indicates that] there is enough to put $1 million in the pocket of every man, woman, and child living in New York City."[4]

That's a lot of treasure. I only have one question: Why should that money be given to *New Yorkers?!* I mean, I'm from North

---

3  I identify with the wisdom of Steve Maraboli when he said about friendships, "Be careful ... not all are what they seem. Some people pretend to be the beach, but they're actually quicksand."

4  *DocWALK: Putting Into Practice What You Say You Believe*, Christian Focus; Revised edition (May 20, 2005), p. 40.

Carolina. Why shouldn't that money go to North Carolinians and Floridians?

There is excitement in a treasure hunt. And we need to dig into God's Word with joy and enthusiasm.

God's Word is also *the believer's food.* It provides manna for our souls. Job tells us that he "treasured the words of God's mouth more than [his] daily food" (Job 23:12) How many of us are starving ourselves by not feasting on God's truth?

> God's Word as the believer's food

My wife of fifty-three years recently said to me that she would like to see less of me. I think she meant it literally. And so, I've been on an intermittent fast for several months. I don't eat anything before 10 AM and can't eat anything after 6 PM. "Aren't you hungry not eating until 10 AM?", my friends ask. And I tell them, "No. But I am suicidal!"

So far I've lost about 20 pounds. My wife could have referred back to our wedding day a bunch of years ago and she could have said, "You know, it just dawned on me that there's 70 pounds of you that I'm not legally married to." But she didn't say that. She didn't need to.

> Taking up our cross daily includes taking up our Bibles daily.

Staying away from physical food to get in better shape is commendable. But fasting from God's Word is insane. What good is a shriveled up soul?

We need to be in God's Word daily. Job, who lost everything in his life and had to endure 30 chapters of poor counseling from his friends, declared, "I have not departed from the commands of his lips; I have treasured the words of his mouth more than my *daily* bread." (23:12). Proverbs 8 tells us that "Blessed are those who listen to me, watching *daily* at my doors, waiting at my doorway." Jesus said, "Whoever wants to be my disciple must deny themselves and take up their cross *daily* and follow me." (Luke 9:23) Taking up our cross daily includes taking up our Bibles daily.

And, when we take our eyes off ourselves, we read that we are to "encourage one another *daily*, as long as it is called 'Today,' so that none of you may be hardened by sin's deceitfulness." (Hebrews 3:13). What better way is there to encourage one another than by sharing what we have gotten from God's Word today?

In many ways God's Word is a kind of *autobiography of God*. The Bible discloses the mind and heart of God for the lost (Matthew 23:37). We learn of His care for His creation (Psalm 145; Acts 14). We read of His joy and delight in those He has redeemed (Psalm 147; Isaiah 62). We get to know God by getting to know His Word.

> God's Word as the autobiography of God.

You may have heard the story about Mrs. McGillicutty who was a very faithful church member. In fact, the Pastor said of her at one mid-week prayer meeting, "We are so blessed to have Mrs. McGillicutty with us tonight. She is so faithful in attending our church every time the doors are open. I think we should honor her tonight by letting her pick out the hymns."

Grey-haired, sweet Mrs. McGillicutty blushed, turned to face the congregation, and said pointing, "I'll take him and I'll take him and I'll take him!"

The Bible is indeed a Him-book. We can choose to live with minimal knowledge of the Lord. Or we can daily pursue a deeper relationship with Him by reading, studying, and meditating on His Word.

I have the deepest respect for the late Dr. J.I. Packer. Part of my reason is that he was kind to endorse several of my books. But, apart from that, he is best know for his classic *Knowing God*. In that critical book he writes,

> What makes life worthwhile is having a big enough objective, something which catches our imagination and lays hold of our allegiance, and this the Christian has in a way that no other

person has. For what higher, more exalted, and more compelling goal can there be than to know God?[5]

> Knowing God allows most of life's problems to fall into place of their own accord.

To the simple question, what ought to be our primary focus in life, Packer writes, "Once you become aware that the main business that you are here for is to know God, most of life's problems fall into place of their own accord."[6]

Although there are many other images used of God's Word, the last we want to consider is that it provides *the divine agenda for the believer*. We read in 2 Timothy 3 that "All Scripture is God-breathed and is useful for teaching, rebuking, correcting and training in righteousness, so that the servant of God may be thoroughly equipped for every good work." (2 Timothy 3:16-17).

> God's Word as the divine agenda

If I am not in the Word daily, it is unlikely that I will be reporting in for today's assignment. If I don't begin my day with the question, "Lord, what would you have for me to do today?", it is quite obvious that I am the master of my fate. I am the captain of my day.

I am not suggesting that reading the Bible daily will give me some kind of supernatural, specific information about exactly what I should do or who I should talk to. The Bible is no magic book. But consulting God's Word every morning recalibrates my mind and my heart to want to do His will and to long to please Him in this new day.

We Christians must repent of our poor views of the Scriptures and wash our minds with the truths of Psalm 119 about the cruciality of the Word of God. We have been deluded into thinking that the Bible is there only to comfort us at funerals or to provide an encouraging verse when we send a birthday gift to a nephew or

---

5   *Knowing God,* J.I. Packer  IVP Books (Downer's Grove, IL, 1973). p. 34.
6   Ibid.

to crochet or decoupage or frame a biblical statement for display in our home.

## Spiritual Surgery

We read in Hebrews 4 that "the word of God is quick, and powerful, and sharper than any two-edged sword, piercing even to the dividing asunder of soul and spirit, and of the joints and marrow, and is a discerner of the thoughts and intents of the heart." (v. 12 KJV)

When we mentally shelve the Word of God, turning to it only in dire emergencies, we are doing great harm to ourselves. God's Word is meant to be studied, meditated on, and carefully applied to every experience we face this day. We assume that a surgeon doesn't need to run to his anatomy textbook so he can find and do surgery on one's appendix. That knowledge should be innate with him, second nature.

> When we mentally shelve God's Word, we do great harm to ourselves.

But that's not the case with the believer and his Bible. It needs to be our constant reference, our daily sourcebook for wisdom and insight, our road map for how we are to navigate our today.

Let's think about that Hebrews 4 text a bit. We read that "the word of God is quick, and powerful, and sharper than any two-edged sword, piercing even to the dividing asunder of soul and spirit, and of the joints and marrow, and is a discerner of the thoughts and intents of the heart." (v. 12 KJV)

Of course, there are some strong reasons why the believer might want to avoid God's Word. We don't naturally want our lives to be cut up by truth, to be pierced by the One who knows our hearts, to have our thoughts and intentions read by God Himself (Hebrews 4:12). But we know that that is exactly what we need if we want to follow the Lord with a whole heart.

God's Word convicts us of sin. It will cause us to face our temptations and either plead with the Lord for strength to resist them or cowardly give in to the promptings of our own evil desires or the enticements of our supernatural enemy.

The Bible will require of us our most diligent mental, emotional, and volitional engagement. Far from being an easy-to-read book, the Bible will insist that we work hard to quarry its meaning. Do you think that you are no longer a student simply because you've earned a high school or college or graduate degree? Think again. If you're a follower of Jesus, you have become a life-long pupil in God's school — and there is a world of homework to get done!

## HOMEWORK

1. Read Chapter Two "The Believer's Authority" in my book *DocWALK: Putting into Practice What We Say We Believe.* Take notes on both wrong views of the Bible and correct ones.
2. Carefully go through all of Psalm 119 this month. It's the longest chapter in the Bible, but gives us amazing statements about the Word of God. List at least five benefits of God's Word every day.
3. Begin an email Bible reading program with several friends. I've been doing this for years and it has been a great encouragement in my life. Choose a book (for example, Ephesians) and read chapter one this week each day. On Sunday send a brief thought to the group of something the Lord gave you from that chapter. Then on Monday begin reading chapter two. And so on.

# CHAPTER THREE:

# WHY SHOULD I CARE?

"To move within the quicksand, a person or object must apply sufficient pressure on the compacted sand to re-introduce enough water to liquefy it. The forces required to do this are quite large: to remove a foot from quicksand at a speed of 1 cm/s would require the same amount of force as that needed to lift a car."[1]

What if there are others who are not even yet close to being in the quicksand? If the quicksand represents the spiritual stuckness of believers, how do you help those who have not yet believed?

Perhaps one reason many Christians get stuck is that their eyes are too often on themselves, their needs, their families, their comfort. But here is where the gospel of Jesus Christ really becomes invasive. If the gospel

"We have in a real sense lost sense of the lostness of the lost." (Dr. Francis Schaeffer)

1   https://www.wikiwand.com/en/Quicksand.

is true, it demands us to open our eyes to those around us who are lost, separated from the love of God, outside the family of God, presently under God's wrath.

## Lost about the Lost?

Dr. Francis Schaeffer said, "We have in a real sense lost sense of the lostness of the lost." Have we? Have you? How lost are people who haven't believed the gospel?

The obvious question to ask is, especially in light of our previous chapter, what does the Bible say? Here the Bible is shockingly clear, giving us **four specific truths about people without Christ**:[2]

1. Those who die without Christ will not survive God's judgment. We read in Psalm 1 that the wicked "will not stand in the judgment" (v. 5). The idea is not that they won't appear at God's judgment, but that they **won't survive His judgment**. We need to lovingly and clearly say to our unsaved friends, "You will stand before God's judgment even if you don't think you will."

> belief in Jesus = no longer condemned
> no belief in Jesus = already condemned

2. The Bible teaches that the wicked (those without Christ) are **already condemned**. John 3:18 says, "Whoever believes in him is not condemned, but whoever does not believe stands condemned already because they have not believed in the name of God's one and only Son." Already condemned. The logic of John 3:18 is straightforward: belief in Him = not (no longer) condemned; not yet believing in Him = already (presently) condemned.

Many people think that the verdict of condemnation or pardon will be decided only at the final judgment seat of God. They envision a massive bronze scale which is filled with our good deeds in one tray and our bad deeds in the other tray. The imagery, of course, is not biblical, for no one can be saved by their good deeds. But if that picture were true, according to the Bible, the good deeds' tray

2   Some of this material is from my book *Unlike Jesus: Let's Stop Unfriending the World.* Energion Publications, 2019.

would be empty, and the sheer gravity of our sins would cause the bad deeds' tray to loudly crash overloaded to the ground, scattering bad deeds everywhere. Scripture even says that all our good works are like filthy rags before God (Isaiah 64:6). The term "filthy rags" is actually the term for menstrual cloths. In other words, no life.

3. What more does the Bible say about the present condition of the lost? Later in John 3 we read, "Whoever believes in the Son has eternal life, but whoever rejects the Son will not see life, for God's wrath remains on them" (v. 36). God's wrath "remains on them." They are already **under the wrath of God**. When you talk to your lost friend, don't you wish that you could be brutally honest and say something like this: "You know, my friend, that God loves you. You know that God gave His Son for your sins. But the bad news of the good news is that you are not in a spiritually neutral condition. Until you trust Christ as your Savior, the wrath of God is presently on you. The only way to extricate yourself from under His wrath is to believe the gospel."

> ## Four truths about the lost:
> 1. won't survive God's judgment
> 2. are already condemned
> 3. are under God's wrath
> 4. are presently the enemy of God

4. We need to help the lost understand that they are **presently enemies of God**. We read in Romans 5, "For if, while we were God's enemies, we were reconciled to him through the death of his Son, how much more, having been reconciled, shall we be saved through his life!" Paul has already said in Romans 5 that Christ died for the ungodly, for us, "when we were still powerless" (v. 6). We were not righteous people who merited Christ's death for us. We read, "But God demonstrates his own love for us in this: While we were still sinners, Christ died for us." (v. 8). Notice the "*while we's*": "while we were enemies," "while we were still powerless," "while we

were still sinners." We must disassociate ourselves from any inkling that anything in our lives commended us to God.

## A Vision Problem

I suspect many of us have a vision problem. We don't look at others as desperately needing the gospel. Our vision is blurred or blinded by many other concerns. There is a fascinating miracle done by the Lord Jesus in Mark 8. We read of a blind man being brought to Jesus, with his friends begging Jesus to touch him (Mark 8:22). Jesus takes him by the hand, leads him outside the village, spits on his eyes, and asks him, "Do you see anything?"

> We often don't see either the trees or the people.

We read that he said, "I see people; they look like trees walking around." Jesus then puts His hands on the man's eyes and "his eyes were opened, his sight was restored, and he saw everything clearly." (v. 25).

This two-stage miracle is unique in the gospels. But isn't it true that we not only don't see people; we often don't even see the trees! How we view others is critical to getting unstuck in our Christian lives.

I've had a recent experience that has made me acutely aware of my vision. My right eye began showing signs of macular degeneration, a condition in which small capillaries leak blood in the eye, eventually leading to blindness. The cure? I had to have several months of injections into my right eye! The first injection was terrifying as you can imagine, but the doctor's assistants did a great job of numbing my eye. All I felt was a slight pinch when the doctor gave me the injection. That first injection was followed by seven more spaced over a year.

When I showed up for my last injection, the doctor looked at the high-res picture of that right eye and said, "You're done. You don't need any more injections. The medicine is working." You can imagine my relief. Now, whenever someone tritely uses the expression "Just stab me in the eye", I don't hesitate to tell them of my real life experience!

## Any Alternatives?

Is that what it's going to take for you and me to start really seeing lost people? As a theologian I wonder if many followers of Jesus inwardly think that those who die without Christ will somehow still be okay or that God will judge them on the basis of their good works or that they will miraculously receive a post-mortem (after-death) opportunity to believe the gospel. None of those options are supported biblically.[1] One receives salvation in this life, on this side of the grave, before death. That's why evangelism and missions are so important!

If I am thoroughly convinced that the gospel is true, that there is only one Savior and His name is Jesus, and that a person is saved only by believing in Him, then I will have to open my eyes to the lost — and really begin to care about reaching them.

The opportunities to really care are all around us. I've dealt with the critical issue of becoming a friend of sinners in my book *Unlike Jesus: Let's Stop Unfriending the World*.[2] We Christians are great at watching Christian movies (the few good ones), listening to Christian music (Lauren Daigle is my favorite), and

> ## Two Kinds of Evangelism:
> 1. becoming a friend of sinners
> 2. single-chance encounters

eating Christian casseroles. We isolate ourselves from lost people and callously just let them continue plummeting to hell.

There are two major kinds of evangelism opportunities. The first is the becoming-a-friend-of-sinners-like-Jesus opportunities.

---

1 For a discussion of the three alternative views to eternal conscious punishment (universalism, annihilationism, and post-mortem conversion), see my book *The Other Side of the Good News: Contemporary Challenges to Jesus' Teaching on Hell* (Christian Focus, 2003).
2 Energion Publications, 2019.

This involves purposing in my heart and pursuing by my choices relationships with those who need the Lord.

There are also what I can single-chance encounters (SCE's) to share the gospel. This may be a conversation in a WalMart, at a child's ball game, in a doctor's office. We believers need to be ready for these potential encounters with those who need Christ. Before I share one of my practices with you, I must say that I'm trying to make myself ready for such connections. I put my phone away and purposely not check my messages or email or play some game on my phone so that I will be ready if an opportunity comes.

One SCE has to do with a promise I made to the Lord a while back. As I was writing this, I just got a phone call. From a telemarketer! Ugh. But I promised the Lord a few months ago that I would try to witness to any telemarketer who called me. Rather than hang up on them or push "delete" when your phone tells you "Possible Spam!", why not share a bit of the gospel with them? Here's how the conversation went a couple of minutes ago:

> **Me:** "Hello?"
> **Telemarketer:** "Mr. Dixon? My name's Brian and I'm from the Auto Warranty Center. How are you?"
> **Me:** "I'm fine, Brian. You?"
> **Telemarketer:** "I'm fine. But it's awfully hot here in California."
> **Me:** "We're getting a lot of rain here in South Carolina. Say, Brian, this could be your most important phone call of the day."
> **Telemarketer:** "Really? Uh, why?"
> **Me:** "Well, I understand how hard it is to do telemarketing. But I'm not really interested in what you're selling. Can I tell you about a promise I made to the Lord a while back?"
> **Telemarketer:** (moment of awkward silence) "Uh, sure."
> **Me:** "Brian, I promised the Lord I would ask any telemarketer that called me if they knew what the gospel is. Do you know what the gospel is?"
> **Telemarketer:** "I WORSHIP SATAN!"
> **Me:** "Really? Why?"
> **Telemarketer:** "Why do YOU worship God?"
> Brian then hung up. On me.

I don't witness to every telemarketer who calls me. Sometimes it's just not convenient for me to take their call. But I wonder: Is *convenience* really a good excuse for not reaching out to the lost?

The church lost a great prophetic voice when Keith Green died in an over-loaded plane years ago. He sang about the lost:

> Do you see? Do you see?
> All the people sinking down
> Don't you care? Don't you care?
> Are you gonna' let them drown?
> How can you be so numb
> Not to care if they come?

## Homework

1. Read my short book *Unlike Jesus: Let's Stop Unfriending the World*. Pay particular attention to the story in Chapter Three "'I Haven't Got Time for the .... ♫' " (a discussion of Luke 7 where Jesus says "Do you see this woman?"). How did Simon the Pharisee need his vision corrected by Jesus?
2. What specifically are you going to do to further develop your passion for lost people? Do you have a prayer hit-list which you use everyday to pray for the Holy Spirit to bring conviction of sin to the hearts of those you love?
3. Some of our witnessing is a one-and-done experience. We might meet someone on a plane or have a brief conversation with our plumber. I call this "evangelism by strafing." In other words, you might not see that person again. I believe God honors a gentle boldness when we step out in faith and share the gospel with a stranger.

Are you bold enough to follow my example when it comes to telemarketers? Do you have an idea for a similar bold effort you can make in single conversation encounters?

# CHAPTER 4:

# WHO SHOULD I IMPACT?

"It is impossible for a human to sink entirely into quicksand due to the higher density of the fluid. Quicksand has a density of about 2 grams per cubic centimeter, whereas the density of the human body is only about 1 gram per cubic centimeter. At that level of density, sinking beyond about waist height in quicksand is impossible. Continued or panicked movement, however, may cause a person to sink further in the quicksand. Since this increasingly impairs movement, it can lead to a situation where other factors such as weather exposure (i.e. sun stroke), dehydration, hypothermia, drowning in a rising tide, or predatory animals may harm a trapped person. Quicksand may be escaped by slow movement of the legs in order to increase viscosity of the fluid, and rotation of the body so as to float in the supine position (lying horizontally with the face and torso facing up)."[3]

---

3   https://blog.supplysideliberal.com/post/2022/2/5/quicksand.

One writer by the name of Joann Ross wrote, "Never get in the middle of someone else's quicksand." I also appreciate the statement by Richelle E. Goodrich who said, "Some decisions in life naturally lead to an unhappy ending, leaving you sinking by degrees in a lake of quicksand. And, unless someone reaches to pull you out, chances are you will drown in the consequences."

How do I help fellow travelers who may or may not be stuck in their spiritual quicksand?

## A Personal Story

I got saved as a teenager, but I don't remember anyone "discipling" me. The closest I got to being discipled was with an elder in our church, Mr. Smith, an old itinerant preacher originally from Ireland. I met with him a couple of times to talk about the Christian life and I think he might have prayed with me. Once. He was a great man of God with a heart for sharing the gospel with the lost.

But I sadly don't recall his sharing his life with me or making any effort to consistently help me advance in my walk with Jesus. I believe he felt that my simply and faithfully attending all the meetings of the church would be enough.

> Discipleship does not happen as a result of spiritual osmosis.

The only other memory I have of Mr. Smith was when my brand new bride and I asked the elders' blessing to go to Germany as missionaries. Mr. Smith withheld his approval, saying that if we weren't doing door-to-door evangelism here in the States, why would we travel overseas to do it? It was a painful experience, but eventually he gave us his blessing. I regret not pursuing deeper conversations with Mr. Smith. I doubt anyone had ever discipled *him*.

I also regret growing up in a church environment that seemed to teach that simply being in the meetings, simply "being under the sound of the Word," was good enough. It was a kind of discipleship by osmosis. Excellent church attendance would lead to Christlikeness.

The sad truth is that most of my teenaged friends -- some who had perfect attendance pins that reached the floor -- abandoned their faith when they went to college.

## Our Default Setting

For many of us our default setting is our own personal comfort. We naturally look after the me-myself-and-mine life that we have. Of course we should care for our own families — and for our own lives. But getting unstuck involves getting some of our vision off ourselves!

Looking outwardly, intentionally asking whose life I might impact for the kingdom, does not come automatically to us. It is a God-given passion to help others in their walk with Christ. It involves opening up our homes, clearing our calendars, limiting our hobbies so that we might influence others for the Lord.

## In-Your-Face Verses

God's Word is clear that my love for Christ must spill over to loving His children. A worthy study is to notice how often the writer of 1 John substitutes "the church" or "one another" for "God" or "Jesus" in his five chapters (see such verses as 1:3; 3:10; 3:14; 3:16; 4:11; 4:20; 5:1).

If I love Him, I will take Jesus' challenge to Peter and apply it to my life: "Feed my lambs. Feed my sheep. Feed my sheep." (John 21:15-18). Bringing spiritual nourishment to others is so critical that Jesus repeats Himself so that Peter gets the message. Where in Scripture are we challenged to disciple others? We must not overlook Jesus' clear marching orders to all believers in Matthew 28.

18 Then Jesus came to them and said, "All authority in heaven and on earth has been given to me. 19 Therefore go and make disciples of all nations, baptizing them in the name of the Father and of the Son and of the Holy Spirit, 20 and teaching them to

> Our task is not simply to produce believers, but disciples.

obey everything I have commanded you. And surely I am with you always, to the very end of the age."

Our task is not simply to produce believers, but disciples. The term "disciple" means "learner." Whatever knowledge I possess as a mature believer must be shared with those who are younger in the faith. We are to "teach the word" (Acts 18:11). We are challenged in 2 Thessalonians 2:15 to communicate the message: "So then, brothers and sisters, stand firm and hold fast to the teachings we passed on to you, whether by word of mouth or by letter."

We are to train younger believers about false teachers who will not spare the flock (Acts 20). Timothy is commanded by the Apostle Paul: "Keep reminding God's people of these things. Warn them before God against quarreling about words; it is of no value, and only ruins those who listen." (2 Timothy 2:14)

> ## Two Growth Metaphors in Hebrews 5:
>
> 1. remedial education
> 2. from milk to meat

## Self-Awareness

Discipling others will often lead us into recognizing we are not where *we* need to be in our own Christian walk. We read the following of the believers in the Epistle to the Hebrews: "In fact, though by this time you ought to be teachers, you need someone to teach you the elementary truths of God's word all over again. You need milk, not solid food!" (Hebrews 5:12)

The writer to the Hebrews is using two metaphors to challenge these believers. First, they are in need of remedial education — summer school! They need to move beyond the basics (without abandoning the basics) into more advanced truths given by the Lord.

The second metaphor might have come across as quite insulting, for the author says that these Christians are like babies who still need the bottle. Their diet needs to move beyond mushed up apple sauce into the meat of God's Word (allow me a little liberty here).

My family and I lived in Canada for about ten years, surrounded by dairy farms. A local TV ad had the tagline, "Milk does the body good!" But a milk only diet leads to milquetoast Christians. [I had to look up the term "milquetoast," by the way. "Milquetoast" is often confused with the term "milk toast." "Milk toast" is a reference to bread which is usually buttered, served in hot milk with sugar or with salt and pepper. It is often given to frail people. "Milquetoast," on the other hand, refers to "a very timid, unassertive, spineless person, especially one who is easily dominated or intimidated." Apparently the term milquetoast came from the comic strip character Caspar Milquetoast, created by the American cartoonist H.T. Webster.][4]

The immaturity of the Hebrew Christians needed milk, not solid food. And the author is not giving them a compliment in writing that.

## Playing with Praying

Can we talk? In the churches that still have mid-week prayer meetings, most of the prayers I hear prayed have to do, not with discipleship, but with health conditions. One church I know has a prayer list on which most of the items are about upcoming surgeries, members' fighting Covid, and information about hospital visits. The one who writes the prayer letter is a medical professional (a dentist) and he doesn't hesitate to go into such medical specifics that I sometimes feel as if I'm looking over the shoulder of the attending physician and reading the patient's medical chart. (I want to cry out, "HOLY HIPPA!")

If one asks how the Apostle Paul prayed for his co-workers and their health, we have only a few statements like: "Drink no longer water, but use a little wine for thy stomach's sake and thine often infirmities." (1 Timothy 5:23 KJV). In 2 Timothy 4 Paul sends greetings to various fellow workers:

"19 Salute Prisca and Aquila, and the household of Onesiph-
orus. 20 Erastus abode at Corinth: *but Trophimus have I left*

---

4   https://www.dictionary.com/browse/milquetoast.

*at Miletum sick.* 21 Do thy diligence to come before winter. Eubulus greeteth thee, and Pudens, and Linus, and Claudia, and all the brethren." (KJV, my emphasis)

Paul obviously didn't apply the truth of prosperity theology for he failed to command Trophimus to name and claim his healing in Jesus!

So, if I'm not to spend an inordinate amount of time and energy praying for the physical well-being of the saints, for what am I to pray? Here's where serious prayer and intentional discipleship intersect.

## Meaty Prayers

> Meaty prayers go beyond physical needs to spiritual growth.

A few years ago I was invited to speak at a men's retreat and I chose as my topic "Several Crucial Questions for REAL Men!" I led the men through Colossians 1:9-14 which reads —

9 For this reason, since the day we heard about you, we have not stopped praying for you. We continually ask God to fill you with the knowledge of his will through all the wisdom and understanding that the Spirit gives, 10 so that you may live a life worthy of the Lord and please him in every way: bearing fruit in every good work, growing in the knowledge of God, 11 being strengthened with all power according to his glorious might so that you may have great endurance and patience, 12 and giving joyful thanks to the Father, who has qualified you to share in the inheritance of his holy people in the kingdom of light. 13 For he has rescued us from the dominion of darkness and brought us into the kingdom of the Son he loves, 14 in whom we have redemption, the forgiveness of sins.

I asked them two questions, "Are you man enough to ask others to pray for you? And do you ask them to pray for the things that are really important?"

I then listed seven items in Paul's prayer for the Colossian believers:

1. that they would lead a worthy life (v. 10);
2. that they would have a desire to please the Lord (v. 10);
3. that they would be fruit-bearing (v. 10);
4. that they would be spiritually growing (v. 10);
5. that they would have the strength to endure (v. 11);
6. that they would be joyfully thankful (v. 12); and
7. that they would rejoice in their rescue (vv. 13-14).

Are you praying for anyone like that? My concern for others, if it is not where it ought to be, will be increased as I spend time praying for them. And praying for their life, their discipleship -- and not just their health!

## Three Levels of Disciples

I cannot say from my own life that I have consistently followed the advice I'm going to give you now. But it is still important and worth listening to. I believe each of us needs three kinds of friends in our lives.

> Three kinds of friends:
> 1. A Paul - an older believer
> 2. A Barnabas - a co-worker
> 3. A Timothy - a younger believer to disciple

Each of us needs a Paul. We need an older believer who can help us in our walk with Christ. Each of us also needs a Barnabas, a co-worker, a fellow-laborer, an equal. And each of us also needs a Timothy. A younger believer into whose life we can pour ours.

## Homework

1. Drop to your knees (if you are able) and ask the Lord to forgive you for not discipling younger believers. And while you're

down there, ask Him to burden your heart with one specific individual you could befriend, pray for, and disciple.

2. Write out a prayer like the one we looked at in Colossians 1 for a younger believer.

3. Pray about starting an online Bible reading group like we discussed in our second chapter.

4. Suggest to your church leaders (your elders especially) the idea that they should set the example and disciple at least one young person every six months.

# Chapter Five:

# Who Do I Need?

If stumbling into quicksand ranks on your list of worries, don't panic. You won't sink in—at least not all the way. Real quicksand is certainly hard to get out of, but it doesn't suck people under the way it always seems to in the movies.

According to a study published in the journal *Nature,* it is impossible for a person immersed in quicksand to be drawn completely under. The fact is, humans float in the stuff.

Researchers in the Netherlands and France studied quicksand, a combination of fine sand, clay, and salt water. At rest, quicksand thickens with time, but it remains very sensitive to small variations in stress. At higher stresses, quicksand liquefies very quickly, and the higher the stress the more fluid it becomes. This causes a trapped body to sink when it starts to move. But a person moving around in quicksand will never go all the way under. The reason is that *humans just aren't dense enough.*"[1]

---

1  My italics. https://www.nationalgeographic.com/science/article/quicksand-science-why-it-traps-how-to-escape.

I don't know — I think we humans can be pretty dense! Especially when it comes to the issue of the church.

## A Personal Word

> Both introverts and extroverts need the local church!

I'm an introvert. I've gone through the personality tests (Enneagram, Myers/Briggs, Briggs & Stratton, etc.) and I test out as an introvert. An "expressive" introvert. But an introvert nonetheless.

What that means is that people pretty much exhaust me. I force myself to go to parties and social gatherings, but only because my dear wife is an extrovert. She loves people. Me, not so much. I'm quite happy being by myself with occasional meetings with my wife and maybe a few grandkids.

I'm overstating this a bit, but introverts like me like quiet, peace, solitude. We spend a lot of time reflecting, listening to soft music (except for early Chicago), and avoiding crowds. My daughter, who is also an introvert, says she's going to get me a T-shirt that reads, "INTROVERTS UNITE! BY YOURSELVES! IN YOUR OWN HOMES!"

I would be perfectly happy living in a cave (with good internet service, of course). But that's not God's best for me.

## Just Jesus and Me![2]

> Overemphasis on individuality and self-awareness can quickly lead to self-idolatry.

One of the popular songs when I was a young believer was entitled "Just Jesus and Me." It came at the height of the "Me" generation and fit in quite nicely with young adults who wanted to "do their own thing."

---

2   The author Steven Wright once said, "When I was a kid we had a sandbox. It was a quicksand box. I was an only child ... eventually."

And we certainly didn't need the stuffy environs of the church to pursue "our own thing."

It seemed that the overemphasis on individuality and self-awareness quickly led to a kind of self-idolatry. And an ignorance of the Scriptures. Afterall, don't we read in Genesis 2 that Adam, before the fall and before the creation of Eve, was declared by God as "lonely?" What?! Wait a minute! He was in the Garden, which had not yet been affected by sin, and was in perfect fellowship with His Creator. And he was lonely?! Yes. And God saw that it was not good.

We need human relationships. And, therefore, we need the church. Now by "the church" I don't mean the universal Body of Christ. Every believer belongs to that by conversion. I mean a local church, a group of believers to which one belongs and to which one contributes.

## The Church — Why Bother?

Philip Yancey, who's written more books than C.S. Lewis and Joel Osteen combined, wrote a small book years ago with the title *Church — Why Bother?* Yancey's book got me thinking — and it seems to me that there are at least four solid reasons to bother with a local church.

> If the Lord Jesus is presently building His church, that truth ought to impact how I relate to the local church's leaders, programs, vision, and foibles.

The first reason is that **I want to join Jesus in His building project**. In a sense the Divine Carpenter has resumed His first occupation — construction. Jesus said that on the rock of Peter's confession of faith in Him, "I will build my church, and the gates of Hades will not overcome it" (Matthew 16:18). Now, one may argue that He was referring to the "universal" church, but how is the universal church seen in this world? Through imperfect, yet authentic, local churches. If the Lord Jesus is presently building His church, that truth ought to impact how I relate to the local church's leaders, programs, vision, and foibles.

What, exactly, is He building? He is building a people for Himself. One of my favorite biblical passages is Titus 2. There we read,

> 11 For the grace of God has appeared that offers salvation to all people. 12 It teaches us to say "No" to ungodliness and worldly passions, and to live self-controlled, upright and godly lives in this present age, 13 while we wait for the blessed hope—the appearing of the glory of our great God and Savior, Jesus Christ, 14 who gave himself for us to redeem us from all wickedness and to purify for himself a people that are his very own, eager to do what is good.

This is a beautiful text about the grace of God which saves, teaches us how to live, and helps us wait for the Lord's return for us. But notice how the Apostle Paul describes the purpose of Christ's giving Himself for us: "who gave himself for us to redeem us from all wickedness and to purify for himself a people that are his very own, eager to do what is good." Christ is redeeming and purifying a people for Himself! That's us! And much of that process happens in connection with one's dedicated commitment to the local church.

The second reason I want to bother with the local church is that the overall tenor of **the New Testament focuses on the community of God's people as gathered in local places.** They are certainly not without their problems, but we have the Corinthian church, the church in Ephesus, the church in Philadelphia, etc. Geographically planted local churches are encouraged, admonished, rebuked even by the New Testament writers. Much of the New Testament is virtually useless if one remains outside Christ's work in the local church.

> Should we strive to be like the First-Century church? Which one?

If the Lord Jesus is presently building His church, that truth ought to impact how I relate to the local church's leaders, programs, vision, and foibles.

I've heard Twenty-First Century Christians say, "Oh, that we were more like the First Century Church!" But wait a minute! Which First Century church do you mean?

Do you mean like the Corinthian church? They had completely ruined both evangelism and discipleship by isolating themselves from lost people and tolerating sin among God's people (see I Cor. 5).

Or do you mean the Galatian church which had deserted "the one who called [them] to live in the grace of Christ and [were] turning to a different gospel" (Gal. 1:6)? These believers were giving in to some false teachers who had infiltrated their ranks and were spying on the freedom they had in Christ in order to make them slaves by putting themselves again under an unbiblical Judaism (Gal. 2:4)!

Perhaps you are thinking about the Ephesian church? We read that it had "left its first love" (Rev. 2:4)? Of course we should seek to emulate the very best of the early church and also recognize where it often went wrong. But we should be involved, connected, committed to what the Lord Jesus is doing in the local church.

The third reason I want to bother with the local church is that **there is much work to be done in both growing believers *in* and winning unbelievers *to* the gospel.** Let's think about these two ideas of *growing in* and *winning to.*

## Growing Believers *In*

Believers in Jesus never move beyond the gospel. We need to preach it to ourselves, reminding our own souls what Christ has done for us. The community of God's people provides numerous opportunities to be reminded of where we were (before Christ) and where we are now. It seems to me that communion, the Lord's Supper, ought to be a weekly reminder of the price that was paid to ransom us from our sins. We are now on the path of becoming like the Savior. The gospel is not just the issue of salvation, but refers to a completely new orientation to all of life.

## Winning Unbelievers To

I have the highest respect for churches which describe themselves as "seeker churches." Their efforts to design services that are geared to the unsaved are commendable.

A few years ago I served on the leadership team of a seeker church. We worked incredibly hard to craft our services to speak

> "Seeker churches" can overlook the needs of the Body.

to those friends who had not yet trusted Christ. We showed our love for the lost in many ways in that church, not the least of which was where we parked. You see, this was in Manitoba, Canada, where the temperature could dip to forty below zero in the winter! And we on the staff reserved the closest parking places at the church for the visitors, not ourselves!

One challenge for seeker churches is that they might lose sight of the needs of the body. We must not overlook the primary responsibility of feeding and growing God's people.

The gospel ought to be made clear whenever the Word is preached to God's people. But it seems that generally evangelism is to happen outside the walls of the local church. And not just by paid staff! Every believer, the Apostle Peter tells us, is to

> be prepared to give an answer to everyone who asks you to give the reason for the hope that you have. But do this with gentleness and respect, 16 keeping a clear conscience, so that those who speak maliciously against your good behavior in Christ may be ashamed of their slander. (1 Peter 3).

The believer in Jesus who doesn't give a whit about the lostness of others is in dire need of repentance!

And it is in the local church where we are to practice the ordinances (some churches call them "sacraments") ordained by God's Word: baptism and the Lord's Supper. Baptizing one's self or serving oneself communion at home in one's pajamas isn't the biblical pattern.

Discipleship must happen in the local church. We need intentional, risky relationships which we develop in order to build up God's people and help one another grow in Christlikeness. Of course that is not confined to the four walls of a physical building we call the church. True discipleship happens through connections that believers pursue with the family of God.

> **Four reasons to bother with the local church:**
> 1. It is what Jesus is building.
> 2. The NT focuses on the community of God's people in local places.
> 3. Much work needs to be done in discipleship and evangelism.
> 4. God has ordained spiritual leaders to care for my soul.

The fourth reason I want to bother with the local church is that **God has ordained spiritual leaders (elders and deacons) who are tasked with caring for my soul!** If I'm disconnected from a local church, I'm removing myself from their encouragement, influence, and correction. The spiritual pastors (elders) are to manage God's household, show hospitality, and encourage sound doctrine and refute those who have theologically strayed (Titus 1). If a believer is disconnected from the local church, he can't be "managed" by godly leaders, partake in intentional hospitality, or be taught and corrected by biblical truth. The Christian who will not put himself under the watch-care of the local church's spiritual leaders will not have the advantage of learning how to have a good reputation with outsiders and may well "fall into disgrace and into the devil's trap." (I Tim. 3:7).

Formal membership may not be outlined in the New Testament, but it is quite clear that every believer is to use his or her gifts to build up others (see Romans 12, I Corinthians 12, Ephesians 4, and I Peter 4), to pray for and submit to godly leaders, and to practice the priorities modeled for us by the early church. Those priorities are set forth in Acts 2:42 where we read, "They devoted themselves to the apostles' teaching and to fellowship, to the breaking of bread and to prayer." Our lives can count for the Kingdom when we devote ourselves to something more than simply our circle of self.

In short, we need truth, friendships, worship, and prayer to thrive in the Christian life. And that's to be found in the local church. Why bother with the local church? Because Christ bothers.

## Homework

1.  Read Yancey's short book *Church: Why Bother?* Discuss that book with a friend and develop a plan to encourage your church leaders in their work.
2.  Read chapter 9 of my book *DocWALK: Putting into Practice What You Say You Believe.* Answer the study questions at the end of that chapter.
3.  Write out a prayer for your pastor or one of the elders of your local church. Pray that prayer each day this week. Consider sharing that prayer with that leader and asking, "How can I specifically pray for you?"

# CHAPTER SIX:

# WHERE DO I START?

"If you do step into quicksand," says study co-author Daniel Bonn, "you'll only sink in a little deeper than your waist. I would say there would be some pressure on the chest, but not enough to cause serious trouble.So how do you get out? Don't ask your friends to tug on you; they're likely to pull you into two pieces if [they] try hard to pull [you] out," said Bonn, a physics professor at the Van der Waals-Zeeman Institute at the University of Amsterdam.

The way to do it is to wriggle your legs around. This creates a space between the legs and the quicksand through which water can flow down to dilate [loosen] the sand," he explained. "You can get out using this technique, if you do it slowly and progressively." [1]

---

1   https://www.nationalgeographic.com/science/article/quicksand-science-why-it-traps-how-to-escape.

Let's imagine that you've read this far in this book and come to realize, "Yes, I'm a bit stuck in my Christian life! Boy, am I glad I bought this book!" (or words to that effect). "But where do I start?", you might ask. That's where the so-called "spiritual disciplines" become very important.

Much has been written about the spiritual disciplines.[2] Richard Foster's work *Celebration of Discipline* is a classic in the field. We are really talking about developing holy habits which grow us in godliness. Some put the disciplines into categories like the following:

> Spiritual Disciplines = holy habits which grow us in godliness.

The Inward Disciplines:
MEDITATION
FASTING
STUDY
SIMPLICITY
SOLITUDE
SERVICE

The Corporate Disciplines:
CONFESSION
WORSHIP
GUIDANCE
CELEBRATION

Let's think about each of these for a few moments.

---

2   The author Alfie Kohn wrote, "However we think about these [long-term] goals, we ought to think about them a lot. They ought to be our touchstone, if only to keep us from being sucked into the quicksand of daily life."

## The Internal Habits

Concerning the "inward disciplines," MEDITATION involves memorizing a passage of Scripture and thinking about it as much as you can. For example, one might memorize Nehemiah 8:10 where he says to the people of Israel, "Go and enjoy choice food and sweet drinks, and send some to those who have nothing prepared. This day is holy to our Lord. Do not grieve, for the joy of the Lord is your strength." Now, you might memorize only the "do not grieve, for the joy of the Lord is your strength," although some might focus on the first part of this verse! The point is that during the day (or during the hard night hours) you can say to yourself, "Do not grieve, for the joy of the Lord is your strength." You might consider reading up on the context of that challenge by Nehemiah to get some background, but the point is to meditate, ruminate, marinate in that verse!

Many of us check our phones when we are standing in line at WalMart, looking at year-old magazines in a doctor's waiting room, or stopped at a red light. How about putting a key Bible verse on your phone that you can look at and think about during those moments?

The next inward discipline is FASTING. I don't believe Scripture commands us to fast (that is to go without food for a particular period of time in order to focus upon the Lord). However, one might quote the Lord Jesus who said in Matthew 9, "How can the guests of the bridegroom mourn while he is with them? The time will come when the bridegroom will be taken from them; then they will fast." (v. 15).

Wait a minute! The bridegroom *has* been taken from us. So voluntary fasting makes sense. Missing a meal to concentrate on God's Word or to prostrate oneself before the Lord in prayer for a serious situation is quite counter-cultural in our frenetic, food-obsessed world, but spiritually healthy.

We learn that fasting is an evidence of returning to the Lord with all one's heart and can include weeping and mourning (Joel 2:12). It is quite possible that a fast, intended to honor the Lord, leaves Him out. Zechariah records the Lord's asking, "Was it really for me that you fasted?" (7:5). God makes it clear in the Old Testament that His kind of fasting, the kind that receives His approval, is one that has specific social implications — loosing the chains of injustice, untying the cords of slavery, and setting the oppressed free (Isaiah 58:6).

The Lord Jesus specifically addressed fasting, castigating Israel's most religious for looking hypocritically somber when they fasted. Fasting is to be a private discipline that the Father who sees what is done in secret will reward (Matthew 6:16-18). In fact, a person is to conceal the fact that they are fasting by putting oil on their head and washing their face (Matthew 6:17). Jesus said, "When you fast, do not look somber as the hypocrites do, for they disfigure their faces to show others they are fasting. Truly I tell you, they have received their reward in full." (Matthew 6:16). Our fasting is to be "unto the Lord."

We learn that the First Century church fasted when they made the important decision to send Saul and Barnabas on their Holy-Spirit-drafted missionary task (Acts 13:2). And Paul and Barnabas appointed elders with prayer and fasting (Acts 14:23).

> **STUDY**

The spiritual discipline of STUDY is very close to my heart as a retired Bible college and seminary teacher. I was a lousy student in high school. And even worse when I went through my first year in Bible college. My attitude toward study was simple. If it was a Monday night, I would flip a quarter. If it landed heads, I'd watch Monday night football till the wee hours. If it landed tails, I'd stay up half the night playing chess with my roommate. But, if it landed on its edge, I'd study for my theology exam the next day!

Then I met my wife to be — and all laziness and joy was gone. She looked at me and said, "You have a theology exam on Friday, right?" I knew it would be a mistake to lie, so I said, "Yes, Dear."

Then she said, "Listen, Buster." (My name has never been 'Buster.' So I realized she was serious). "If you do not ace your theology exam on Friday, I will not date you on Saturday." I aced the exam on Friday, got on the Dean's list thereafter, and completed a Master's and a Doctorate over the next few years. All because of romantic blackmail.

Believers in Jesus — whether they recognize it or not — are life-long, even eternity-long, students! We will forever be studying the character of our God. So let's get started now.

I have a cartoon of Calvin and Hobbes in which Calvin is waiting for the school bus in a downpour. He asks, "Why in the world am I waiting in the pouring rain for the school bus to take me somewhere I don't even want to go?" He then says, "I go to school, but I never learn what I want to know." Our problem is that *we don't know what we need to learn.* That's why we have trained preachers and teachers and Bible study leaders to help us.

As a young believer I remember some of the older Christians quoting 2 Timothy 2:15 from the King James Bible to me. That verse says, "Study to shew thyself approved unto God, a workman that needeth not to be ashamed, rightly dividing the word of truth." They used this verse to encourage the youth to be better students. However, I learned much later that the term "study" is actually a word which means "to do your best", "to make haste", "to give diligence to." But looking more carefully at the verse, the challenge is indeed to be a serious workman in God's Word! One translation renders this verse as: "Be diligent to present yourself before God as one tried and true, an unashamed worker, correctly handling the word of truth." One must be a diligent student of the Bible in order to correctly "handle" it.

Life can get quite complicating, can't it? The spiritual discipline of SIMPLICITY involves the elements of creating margins in our lives, learning to say no when appropriate, and focusing our attention on the Lord instead of the things of this world. Creating some space for ourselves can be a

SIMPLICITY

challenge, but a healthy life needs alone time as well as interaction time with others. A great teacher of preachers once said, "Men, learning to say 'no' will do you more good than learning Latin!" Active, involved believers are often the first ones to be asked to get involved in another ministry or take on some additional church duties. Sometimes the most spiritual thing we can do is say, "No. I'm quite involved right now."

Focusing on the Lord is the third element of SIMPLICITY. We speak with Him in prayer and He speaks to us through His Word. We realize that we are responsible for our thought lives and we ask for help in applying the challenge of Philippians 4 where the Apostle Paul writes, "Finally, brothers and sisters, whatever is true, whatever is noble, whatever is right, whatever is pure, whatever is lovely, whatever is admirable—if anything is excellent or praiseworthy—think about such things." (v. 8).

**SOLITUDE** The simple practice of SOLITUDE is a piece of cake for an introvert like me. Introverts like to be alone. But biblical solitude is much more than aloneness. It is a concerted time with the Lord, an intentional distancing from others and the distractions of this world to simply spend time with the God who wants to spend time with us.

**SERVICE** The great theologian Bob Dylan said, "You gotta serve somebody!" SERVICE is the practice of thinking of others before ourselves, asking how we might encourage another in their Christian life. Ephesians 2 says we've been "appointed to good works." And those works are to be done for the sake of others.

## The Outward Habits

**CONFESSION** The so-called corporate disciplines have to do with the Body of Christ, the church. We are to engage in CONFESSION as James says: "Confess your faults one to another, and pray one for another, that ye may be healed. The effectual fervent prayer of a righteous man availeth much." (James 5:16, KJV) Someone has said that confession is good for the soul, but bad for the reputation. But protecting one's reputation, instead of admitting and dealing with sin, keeps us from finding forgiveness and cleansing from the Lord (often mediated through God's people).

Of course we are to give ourselves to WORSHIP and that should regularly happen with God's people. We were never intended to restrict our worship to our individual lives.

**WORSHIP**

Has it dawned on you that much of what the Holy Spirit does He does *through* God's people? I've examined many of the ministries of God the Holy Spirit and most of them seem to be done mediately not immediately. "Mediately" refers to how He uses the people of God as the means or avenue of His work. "Immediately" refers to directness, not to time. GUIDANCE is often given by the Holy Spirit as He speaks to God's people through God's people.

**GUIDANCE**

The one outward discipline that Christians seem to have a hard time practicing is CELEBRATION. Like the older brother of the prodigal son (Luke 15), we don't allow ourselves to get caught up in the joyful excitement of someone coming back to the Lord. But we should. When God says "Party!", we need to party. We need to celebrate lost loved ones who get saved and wayward believers who get spiritually restored.

**CELEBRATION**

## HOMEWORK:

1. Read a book like Foster's *Celebration of Discipline* or *Spiritual Disciplines for the Christian Life* by Donald Whitney and J.I. Packer. Discuss your book with another believer.

2.  Find an accountability partner with whom you can work on a couple of the inward disciplines. Check up on each other's progress and consistently pray for one another.

3.  Discuss one of the corporate disciplines with some of the leaders in your local church. Ask how you can help them improve those disciplines among the people of God.

# CHAPTER SEVEN:

# HOW DOES THIS END?

You are no longer in the quicksand, spiritually speaking, because you're now facing the end of the world! The battle is over. Jesus is wrapping up history. So what now? With you? The very possibility of being stuck is now gone! When Jesus completes human history, He will also wrap our personal struggles with sin, our efforts at sanctification, and our sometimes meager movements toward godliness. We will become like the Lord Jesus, an event theologians call "glorification." But, first, there *will* be a judgment!

## Different Judgments?

Many Christians believe that there will be one massive judgment before God at the end of time. Some draw that conclusion based on the judgment of the sheep and the goats found in Matthew 25. There we read —

31 "When the Son of Man comes in his glory, and all the angels with him, he will sit on his glorious throne. 32 All the nations will be gathered before him, and he will separate the people one from another as a shepherd separates the sheep from the goats. 33 He will put the sheep on his right and the goats on his left. 34 "Then the King will say to those on his right, 'Come, you who are blessed by my Father; take your inheritance, the kingdom prepared for you since the creation of the world. 35 For I was hungry and you gave me something to eat, I was thirsty and you gave me something to drink, I was a stranger and you invited me in, 36 I needed clothes and you clothed me, I was sick and you looked after me, I was in prison and you came to visit me.'

37 "Then the righteous will answer him, 'Lord, when did we see you hungry and feed you, or thirsty and give you something to drink? 38 When did we see you a stranger and invite you in, or needing clothes and clothe you? 39 When did we see you sick or in prison and go to visit you?'

40 "The King will reply, 'Truly I tell you, whatever you did for one of the least of these brothers and sisters of mine, you did for me.'

> ## The Sheep and the Goats (Mt. 25):
> A separation of all of humanity

41 "Then he will say to those on his left, 'Depart from me, you who are cursed, into the eternal fire prepared for the devil and his angels. 42 For I was hungry and you gave me nothing to eat, I was thirsty and you gave me nothing to drink, 43 I was a stranger and you did not invite me in, I needed clothes and you did not clothe me, I was sick and in prison and you did not look after me.'

44 "They also will answer, 'Lord, when did we see you hungry or thirsty or a stranger or needing clothes or sick or in prison, and did not help you?'

45 "He will reply, 'Truly I tell you, whatever you did not do for one of the least of these, you did not do for me.'

46 "Then they will go away to eternal punishment, but the righteous to eternal life."[1]

What does Matthew 25 teach about the final judgment? We learn that there is a "glorious throne" upon which the Son of Man will sit when He comes in His glory (v. 31). He will be the Judge (John 5:22 says, "the Father judges no one, but has entrusted all judgment to the Son"). Those who appear before Him are referred to as "all the nations" (v. 32). This certainly sounds all-inclusive.

We then learn that **a great separation** will take place. Like a shepherd separating the sheep from the goats, the sheep will be put on His right and the goats on His left (v. 33). Some websites explain why sheep and goats are often separated from each other. They have different needs. Sheep are highly sensitive to some goat-feeds. They have different fighting styles. And goats can contract a serious disease from sheep.

However, the issue in Matthew 25 concerns *spiritual* sheep and goats. Here the sheep and the goats stand for people ("all the nations"). Why does the shepherd separate them? The passage clearly tells us.

## The King Addresses the Sheep (vv. 34-40)

The King (presumably the Son of Man, Jesus, who is sitting on His glorious throne) will address those on His right, the sheep (vv. 34-40). What does He say to them? He addresses them as "you who are blessed by my Father." He tells them to take their inheritance, "the kingdom prepared for you since the creation of the world" (v. 34).

The King then explains why they are worthy to receive this kingdom. He says (1) He was hungry and the sheep gave Him something to eat. (2) He was thirsty and the sheep gave Him something to drink. (3) He was a stranger and the sheep invited Him in. (4) He needed clothes and the sheep clothed Him. (5) He was

---

1   One must, simply must, listen to Keith Green's song "The Sheep and the Goats" found at: https://youtu.be/y8OhIMwMicE.

sick and the sheep looked after Him. (6) He was in prison and the sheep came and visited Him. These six categories of "works" are commended by the Lord. (vv. 34-36).

The sheep — now called "the righteous" — ask the King "When did we see you in need of those six works?" (vv. 37-40) The King answers and says, "Truly I tell you, whatever you did for one of the least of these brothers and sisters of mine, you did for me" (v. 40).

## The King Addresses the Goats (vv. 41-45)

The King's words to the goats begin not with the "come" He spoke to the sheep, but with the awful word "depart!" (v. 41). And He refers to the goats as "you who are cursed." They are not "blessed by the Father" as are the sheep (v. 34).

And the goats are told in no uncertain terms the destination to which they should depart: "depart from me . . . into the eternal fire prepared for the devil and his angels" (v. 41). There could be no greater opposite in these words to the blessing words given to the sheep (to "take your inheritance, the kingdom prepared for you since the creation of the world") (v. 34).

### A Comparison of the Sheep and Goats in Matthew 25:31-46

|  | THE SHEEP (on His right) | THE GOATS (on His left) |
|---|---|---|
| How are they addressed by the Lord | "you who are blessed" (v. 34) "the righteous" (v. 46) | "you who are cursed" (v. 41) |
| His invitation | "Come . . . take your inheritance, the kingdom prepared for you since the creation of the wold" (v. 34) | "Depart from me . . . into the eternal fire prepared for the devil and his angels" (v. 41) |
| His judgment | His commendation (vv. 35-40) | His condemnation (vv. 41-45) |
| His conclusion | "but the righteous to eternal life" (v. 46) | "they will go away to eternal punishment" (v. 46) |

It seems reasonable to conclude from Matthew 25 that one's works are extremely important when it comes to final judgment. However, they are the evidence of salvation and not its means.

But we also need to be reminded of Matthew 7 where Jesus says,

> 21 "Not everyone who says to me, 'Lord, Lord,' will enter the kingdom of heaven, but the one who does the will of my Father who is in heaven. 22 On that day many will say to me, 'Lord, Lord, did we not prophesy in your name, and cast out demons in your name, and do many mighty works in your name?' 23 And then will I declare to them, 'I never knew you; depart from me, you workers of lawlessness.'"

So here in Matthew 7 we have some who presumably have indeed done works in the name of Jesus (unlike the goats of Matthew 25). But they are rejected by the Lord because He "never knew them." (v. 23). This passage, like many others (for example John 6 where we read: "Then they asked him, 'What must we do to do the works God requires?' Jesus answered, "The work of God is this: to believe in the one he has sent.'") clearly teach that getting into heaven is a result of *knowing Jesus* and *believing* in Him! It seems quite possible that some will have the ability to prophesy, cast out demons, and even do mighty works in the name of Jesus, but not know Him! According to this text, they are called "workers of lawlessness" and are thrust out from the presence of the Lord.[2]

On the surface Matthew 25 which we considered sounds like there will be one massive judgment for all people. However, could this description of the separation of the sheep and the goats be a preliminary judgment which then leads to the next two judgments we will consider?

> Mt. 25- No works but no faith in Christ
> Mt. 7 - works but no faith in Christ

---

2   The idea of exclusion or banishment from God's presence is a common theme concerning "the wicked." We read in Psalm 125- 4 Lord, do good to those who are good, to those who are upright in heart. 5 But those who turn to crooked ways the Lord will banish with the evildoers."

Many believers hold that there is a difference between the Great White Throne Judgment and the Judgment Seat of Christ. Let's look at the primary text on the Great White Throne Judgment.

## The Great White Throne Judgment

We have an overarching statement about final judgment in Hebrews 9:27 where the writer says, "Just as people are destined to die once, and after that to face judgment . . ." But the primary text for the Great White Throne Judgment is Revelation 20:11-15. There we read —

> 11 Then I saw a great white throne and him who was seated on it. The earth and the heavens fled from his presence, and there was no place for them. 12 And I saw the dead, great and small, standing before the throne, and books were opened. Another book was opened, which is the book of life. The dead were judged according to what they had done as recorded in the books. 13 The sea gave up the dead that were in it, and death and Hades gave up the dead that were in them, and each person was judged according to what they had done. 14 Then death and Hades were thrown into the lake of fire. The lake of fire is the second death. 15 Anyone whose name was not found written in the book of life was thrown into the lake of fire.

At first glance Revelation 20 sounds like all of humanity is gathered before the Great White Throne. There could be no greater cataclysmic event than this one, for we read that "the earth and the heavens fled from his (the one seated on the great white throne) presence, and there was no place for them" (v. 11). Earth and the heavens are *removed* as the ruler of the universe prepares to pronounce judgment.

Is all humanity gathered here? We read in verse 12 that "the dead, great and small" are standing at that judgment. From whence come these "dead"? Verse 13 says the dead had been in the sea and that even "death and Hades" gave up the dead that were "in them" (v. 13). This is a strong text indicating that those who die unsaved go to a place called "Hades," which is a real, although not their final, destination.[3]

What happens at this Great White Throne Judgment? Clearly we are told that "books" are opened (vv. 12-15), including "the book of life" (v. 12). These books are the standard by which God metes out judgment. "The dead," we are told, "were judged according to what they had done as recorded in the books" (v. 12). That idea of being judged according to what one had done is repeated in the next verse (v. 13).

> "Anyone whose name was not found written in the book of life was thrown into the lake of fire." (Rev. 20:15)

The most critical book that is opened, it seems, is "the book of life." If a person's name is not found in the book of life, their eternal fate could not be more ominous. We read, "Anyone whose name was not found written in the book of life was thrown into the lake of fire."

We do not read here in Revelation 20 about the righteous being welcomed into heaven. The implication in the text is that this is a judgment of all the unsaved, for none of their names are in the book of life. The focus is on the dead whose works are reviewed. But the critical, final factor is whether or not their names are "written in the book of life" (v. 15).

When I was a student in Bible college, there was an elder in my home church who would write me once in a while and send me a small check. I appreciated his notes of encouragement. But he also had the habit of putting a Bible reference at the end of his note or card and it was always Revelation 20:15 which reads, "Anyone whose name was not found written in the book of life was thrown into the lake of fire"! I don't think he was questioning my salvation. I think that such a verse was expressing his gratitude to the Lord for his salvation!

---

3   The first book I wrote is called *The Other Side of the Good News* and sets forth the biblical case for everlasting punishment for the lost.

## The Judgment Seat of Christ

There seems to be evidence from our look at Matthew 25 that there will be one great time of judgment for all humanity. But what do we learn of the judgment seat of Christ?

In Romans 14 we read the following: "You, then, why do you judge your brother or sister? Or why do you treat them with contempt? For we will all stand before God's judgment seat." (v. 10). The context of Romans 14 has to do with how we treat our brothers and sisters in Christ. Granted, the Apostle Paul does quote from Isaiah 45:23 when he writes, "It is written: 'As surely as I live,' says the Lord, every knee will bow before me; every tongue will acknowledge God.'" This sounds like a judgment of all humanity, doesn't it? Paul then writes, "So then, each of us will give an account of ourselves to God" (v. 12).

However, the primary passage for the judgment seat of Christ appears to be 2 Corinthians 5. There we read,

> 6 Therefore we are always confident and know that as long as we are at home in the body we are away from the Lord. 7 For we live by faith, not by sight. 8 We are confident, I say, and would prefer to be away from the body and at home with the Lord. 9 So we make it our goal to please him, whether we are at home in the body or away from it. 10 For we must all appear before the judgment seat of Christ, so that each of us may receive what is due us for the things done while in the body, whether good or bad.

The context of 2 Corinthians 5, it seems to me, is clearly that of believers only.

> The sheep will appear before the Judgment Seat of Christ (2 Cor. 5)

## Conclusion:

While it is certainly a debate worth having, there appears to be some evidence that the Great White Throne Judgment will be for unbelievers whose names don't appear in the book of life. It also seems reasonable that the believers, "the sheep" (Matthew 25), will then appear before the Judgment Seat of Christ.

## The Issue of Rewards

As we conclude our study about getting stuck in the Christian life, we want to emphasize the biblical hope of future rewards in Christ. The idea of seeking to live so that we will be rewarded by the Lord isn't unspiritual; it is not mercenary. We have ample evidence in the Word that God is a rewarder of those who serve Him.

Both Matthew chapters 5 and 6 speak to this issue of rewards. For example, we learn in Matthew 5 —

1. We have nine circumstances in which a believer is called "blessed" (vv. 1-11). We are then told in verse 12, "Rejoice and be glad, because great is your **reward** in heaven . . ."

2. We are to let our lights shine before others, so "that they may see your good deeds and glorify your Father in heaven" (v. 16). That's a reward worth working toward!

3. We are told that "whoever practices and teaches these commands will be called great in the kingdom of heaven" (v. 19). I'm not looking to be called great in heaven, but that's what the text says.

4. Concerning our enemies, we read, "If you love those who love you, what **reward** will you get? Are not even the tax collectors doing that?" (v. 46).

We then learn in Matthew 6 —

1. If you practice your righteousness in front of others, "you will have no **reward** from your Father in heaven." (v. 1).
2. Concerning giving to the needy, we read — 2 "So when you give to the needy, do not announce it with trumpets, as the hypocrites do in the synagogues and on the streets, to be honored by othe rs. Truly I tell you, they have received their **reward** in full. 3 But when you give to the needy, do not let your left hand know what your right hand is doing, 4 so that your giving may be in secret. Then your Father, who sees what is done in secret, will **reward** you."

5. Concerning prayer, we are not to be like the hypocrites who pray to be seen by others. Jesus says, "Truly I tell you, they have received their **reward** in full" (v. 5). Praying in secret is seen by your Father, and He "will **reward** you" (v. 6).

6. Those who fast to be seen by others "have received their **reward** in full" (v. 16). Fasting in secret will result in your Father **rewarding** you (v. 18).

7. We are store up for ourselves treasures in heaven where moths and vermin can't destroy and thieves can't break in and steal (vv. 19-21).

8. Lastly in Matthew 6, we are told to "seek first his kingdom and his righteousness, and all these things will be given to you as well." (v. 33).

There is so much more in the Scriptures about the believer and the rewards promised to him. For example, we learn in I Corinthians 3 that "they will each be **rewarded** according to their own labor" (v. 8) and that one's salvation is not dependent on one's faithfulness for there we have a man who wasted his Christian life, but "he himself shall be saved" (v. 15). We are told that "If what has been built survives, the builder will receive a **reward**" (v. 14).

## A few summary statements:

1. Our **reward** can be great in heaven (Luke 6:23).
2. We know the Lord will **reward** each one "for whatever good they do, whether slave or free" (Ephesians 6:8).
3. We will receive "an inheritance from the Lord as a **reward**" (Col. 3:24).
4. The Lord **rewards** those "who earnestly seek him" (Hebrews 11:6).
5. Moses "regarded disgrace for the sake of Christ as of greater value than the treasures of Egypt, because he was looking ahead to his **reward**." (Hebrews 11:26).
6. A time will come when the Lord will judge the dead and **reward** His servants and all who revere His name (Rev. 11:18).

7.  We learn in the very last chapter of the book of Revelation that Jesus will say, ""Look, I am coming soon! My **reward** is with me, and I will give to each person according to what they have done." (Rev. 22:12).

## Epilogue:

Spiritual stuckness is real, but redeemable. The various quicksands of this world — and of our own wayward desires and priorities — can prevent us from moving on in godliness.

But, praise God!, He has made provision in His Word and in His people to help stuck people like you . . . and me. Don't stay in your quicksand. And be aware that it will always be there — until Christ returns — for you to wander back into it.

Living for the Lord is a daily choice. But we long for the day when He will say to each of us, "Well done, good and faithful servant! You have been faithful with a few things; I will put you in charge of many things. Come and share your master's happiness!" (Matthew 25:41).

# "Self Soul-Care: A Challenge for Self-Directed Learning"

Larry Dixon, Ph.D.

A recent visit to a Chick-Fil-a restaurant reminded me of a central issue in the Christian life. A cardboard advertisement on the table mocked boring breakfasts. Cereals with names like "Frosted Monotony," "Stale Puffs," and "Bland-O's" did the trick, suggesting that such breakfasts provide half the flavor and are "chock full of stale mediocrity." How like some of our experiences in living out the Christian life! Part of the solution to stuck, stale spirituality is self soul-care.

In speaking of self soul-care, we are not suggesting that we are to direct our learning towards ourselves or that we should neglect godly teachers of the Word of God. Rather, we mean that we must stop blaming others for our lack of spiritual growth. We must take responsibility for where we are in our Christian lives.

The great theologian Calvin (of Calvin and Hobbes) illustrates this point. Calvin says to Hobbes, "Nothing I do is my fault. My family is dysfunctional and my parents won't empower me. Consequently, I'm not self-actualized." He continues, "My behavior is addictive functioning in a disease process of toxic codependency. I need holistic healing and wellness before I'll accept any responsibility for my actions!" Hobbes says to him, "One of us needs to stick his head in a bucket of ice water." To which Calvin replies, "I love the culture of victimhood." We all do, don't we?

May I suggest that we not only need to stop blaming others, we also must reject any notion of spiritual osmosis. We do not grow in the Christian life simply by attending meetings and "being under the sound of the Word." Our problem, if I may be so blunt, is that we hate doing homework, we avoid studying at all costs, and we're not sure we want to take responsibility for our own lives.

## I. Some of the Problems We Face in Self Soul-Care:

Before we look at two primary biblical passages, let me suggest three problems which keep us from engaging in serious, strategic self soul-care. The first I call voluntary illiteracy. Functional illiteracy refers to those who want to read but can't. Voluntary illiteracy refers to those who can read, but don't. John Wesley said, "It cannot be, that the people should grow in grace, unless they give themselves to reading. A reading people will always be a knowing people."

A second problem in self soul-care I call a "spoon-feeding frenzy." Sharks go on a feeding frenzy. I believe many of us Christians go on a spoon-feeding frenzy. That is, we live off second- hand Bible study, second-hand devotions, second-hand living out the Christian life.

A third problem why we don't fully engage ourselves in self soul-care is that there are few challenges to do so. Many of us have no non-Christian friends who ask us hard questions. We also frequently lack any exposure to genuine unbelief. I am convinced that, for those who have been Christians for a while, reading what I call "books that will boil your blood before you get past the preface" will challenge us and make us grow. Books like Charles Templeton's *Farewell to God* or Richard Dawkins' *The God Delusion* will get us digging into the Word of God for ourselves.

## II. Two Texts That Challenge Us to Self Soul-Care:

Paul writes to the Colossians: "So then, just as you received Christ Jesus as Lord, continue to live in him, rooted and built up in him, strengthened in the faith as you were taught, and overflowing with thankfulness." (Col. 2:6-7). Note the two stages of the Christian life: (1) receiving Christ Jesus as Lord, and (2) continuing to live in Him. In fact, the "continuing to live in Him" is actually a command: "continue to live in Him." How can I know if I am continuing to live in Him? Paul gives us three tests: (1) I will be rooted and built up in Him; (2) I will be strengthened in the faith I was taught; and, (3) I will be overflowing with thankfulness. Quite simply, I will be growing, glowing, and overflowing.

But the primary text I'd like to look at with you is a well-known passage. Would you do me (and you) a favor? Pretend that you've never seen the following passage before. Ready? Here's a passage I'll bet you've never seen before:

Come to me, all you who are weary and burdened, and I will give you rest. Take my yoke upon you and learn from me, for I am gentle and humble in heart, and you will find rest for your souls. For my yoke is easy and my burden is light. (Matthew 11:28-30)

What a great text! Never seen it before? Well, it fits our discussion quite nicely. May I suggest the following outline:

I. The Invitation (v. 28)
II. The Invitees (v. 28)
III. The Promise (v. 28)
IV. The Commands (v. 29)
V. The Explanation (vv. 29-30)

Let's look at these fantastic statements from the Lord Jesus. First of all, the Invitation (v. 28). Biblical Christianity begins with an invitation. John Stott discusses how an invitation often has the cryptic letters "RSVP" at the bottom of the invitation. This is a French request to "please reply to the invitation." Stott says, "There was a couple who found political asylum in this country during the Second World War. They came from East or Central Europe. And they were not really well-versed in Western culture. One day they received an invitation to a wedding. And there, at the bottom of the invitation, were those cryptic letters: RSVP. And in his thick European accent, the husband said, "VIF, VAT does it mean? 'RSVP'? I don't know VAT it means!" So they thought for a while and then suddenly inspiration dawned on him. And the husband said, "VIF. I know VAT it means! It means '**R**EMEMBER **S**END **V**EDDING **P**RESENTS!" Many fail to understand that Christianity begins with an invitation, not a demand. It is an invitation, please notice, not to a philosophy, or a religion, but to a person. Here's a tough question for us all: Is it possible to be in this thing called Christianity but have little to do personally with Jesus Himself?

Let's now notice the Invitees (v. 28). Jesus' invitation is clearly to those who "are weary and burdened." The term "weary" refers to those who are physically tired or emotionally discouraged. The word "burdened" can mean weighed down with troubles. Those who are not weary or burdened aren't being invited!

Jesus' promise (v. 28) is quite simple: "I will give you rest." There are several possibilities as to the meaning of this rest which Jesus promises. This word is used in Mark 6:31 to refer to physical rest, in 2 Corinthians 7:5 to a rest from trials, and in I John 3:19-20 to a rest of heart. I would suggest that the meaning is most likely a rest from one's own works. If the rest that Jesus promises refers to the rest of salvation in Him, then His invitation is to those who are tired of trying to earn their own salvation apart from Christ. We read in Hebrews 4:10 that "anyone who enters God's rest also rests from his own work, just as God did from his."

We next notice the two commands (v. 29) which Jesus issues to those who come to Him. His first command is to "take my yoke upon you . . ." What an interesting juxtaposition: He has just promised rest in verse 28. Now He commands those He has invited to voluntarily take upon themselves His yoke, a symbol of work. Jesus does not promise unemployment to those who come to Him. I understand that the great American humorist Will Rogers said during the Depression, "100,000 Americans ain't working, but, thank the Lord, at least they've got jobs!"

Jesus invites His followers to become co-laborers with Him in the work of the Kingdom (see also I Cor. 3:9; Col. 4:11). When I was a teenager, "Dobie Gillis" was a popular TV program. Dobie's best friend, Maynard G. Krebbs, was a hippie-like character who mooched off others. Whenever he heard the word "work" he would, in today's vernacular, freak and shout, "WORK! *WORK?*" There is work for each of us to do -- and Jesus is inviting us to volunteer for that work.

The second command which Jesus gives to those who come to Him is also in verse 29: "and learn from me." Here He invites us not to labor but to learning. What in the world makes us think that learning is optional? Our lives—as well as our eternity—will be spent learning from Him and about Him!

I am again helped on this point by a profound Calvin and Hobbes cartoon strip. Calvin is in his rain gear, waiting for the school bus, and he says, "Why in the world am I waiting in the pouring rain for the school bus to take me somewhere I don't even want to go?" The next frame shows the rain coming down in buckets on him as he stands beside his mailbox at the street. In the last frame he says, "I go to school, but I never learn what I want to know."

Jesus invites all of us to "learn from me." Flannery O'Connor, who lived long before Calvin and Hobbes came on the scene, actually attacks Calvin's problem directly when she writes, "The high-school English teacher will be fulfilling his responsibility if he furnishes the student a guided opportunity, through the best writing of the past, to come, in time, to an understanding of the best writing of the present. And if the student finds that this is not to his taste? Well, that is regrettable. Most regrettable. **His taste should not be consulted; it is being formed."**

That's exactly right. When we come to Jesus to learn from Him our tastes are not being consulted. They are being formed. Our problem is we don't know what it is that we need to know. It is the teacher who sets the educational agenda. As a seminary teacher, I'm deeply committed to training students for ministry. The issue is not so much what am I teaching as what are my students learning? The fundamental idea in the word "disciple" is not discipline, but learner. What's involved in being a learner? Certainly an attitude of wanting to learn, a need to grow in knowledge, and a curiosity (an eagerness to learn). I don't know about you, but I am alarmed at what I perceive to be the lack of curiosity on the part of many Christians. Dorothy Parker has said, "The cure for boredom is curiosity. There is no cure for curiosity."

Two other elements are involved in learning: a teacher and basic study skills. We must resist the seduction of our post-modern culture that suggests that no one has the answers, that no story is absolute, that no teacher has authority. Teaching is highly esteemed in the Scriptures; those who would be elders must be "able to teach" (I Tim. 3:2). I am convinced that many sincere believers in our churches could use a refresher course on basic study skills. How does one study a passage of Scripture? How does one develop an outline? How can one improve his or her reading skills?

When I was a student at Emmaus Bible College (shortly after all the dinosaurs had become extinct), I remember my problem with learning. I made C's and D's. You see, I had an attitude. Not a good attitude either. If I had an exam on Tuesday, on Monday night I would flip a quarter. I said to myself, "If it lands on heads, I'll watch 'Monday Night Football' until the wee hours of the morning. If it lands on tails, I'll play chess with my roommate for several hours. But if it lands on its edge, I'll study for my exam!"

My life changed dramatically when my wife-to-be came to Emmaus my second year. She saw great potential in me and decided to do something to inspire me. She said, "You are capable of doing so much better academically than you are doing." "Yes, Dear," I said, half-heartedly agreeing with her. "No, I mean it. In fact," she said, "I will not date you this coming Saturday if you do not ace your doctrine exam this Friday!" Romantic blackmail. It worked! I aced that exam and was on the dean's list every semester thereafter. Anybody love you enough to romantically blackmail you into becoming a better learner at the feet of Jesus?

Please notice that Matthew 11:28-30 concludes with Jesus' explanation. Jesus says, ". . . for I am gentle and humble in heart, and you will find rest for your souls. For my yoke is easy and my burden is light." We learn about Christ's character in verse 29—He is gentle and humble in heart. Matthew quotes Isaiah 42:3 when he says in his next chapter about the Messiah, "A bruised reed shall he not break, and smoking flax shall he not quench, till he send forth judgment unto victory." (Matthew 12:20). This is certainly a clear reference to His gentleness. Christ again guarantees rest in verse 29, a soul-rest which makes perfect sense to those who commit to His labor and learning from Him. Jesus then speaks of His uniqueness in verse 30 when He says, "For my yoke is easy and my burden is light."

Have you found His yoke to be easy and His burden to be light? Some scholars suggest that the meaning of His yoke being "easy" is that it would be non-chaffing. One says that perhaps Joseph's carpenter shop had a sign over it that read, "We make non-chaffing yokes." The point is that Jesus knows what we can handle -- and He crafts individual yokes for each of us. How about His burden? I must admit that sometimes I feel that His burden is anything but light. I can easily become overwhelmed with my burden for this lost world. But when I allow my burden to overshadow His strength in my life, I have taken on too much.

A burdened heart is a healthy heart, if that burden is from the Lord. May the prayer of your life and mine be, "Lord, I want to grow in grace, and not groan in disgrace."

# BOOKS BY LARRY DIXON

*Abandon All Hope* (a novel) (self-published; 2013)

*After This Life . . . What? An Examination of Several Religious Views of the Afterlife* (self-published; 2016)

*BLESS-ED! 52 Weekly Blessings You Have As a Believer — and How to Help Your Lost Friend Find Theirs* (Christian Focus, 2023)

*DocDevos: Ten Minute Daily Devotionals on the Great Doctrines of the Christian Faith* (Christian Publications; 2002)

*DocTalk: A Fairly Serious Survey of All That Theological Stuff* (Christian Focus; 2001)

*DocWalk: Putting into Practice What You Say You Believe* (Christian Focus; 2005)

*"Farewell, Rob Bell": A Biblical Response to <u>Love Wins</u>* (self-published; 2011)

*Farewell, Rob Bell -- 2nd Edition: Includes a Review of "What We Talk about When We Talk about God"* (self-published, 2013)

*The Forgotten Third: Developing a Biblical Relationship with God the Holy Spirit* (Energion, 2022)

*Friends Don't Let Friends . . . Die! A 1st Person Account of the Raising of Lazarus from the Dead. Me* (self-published, 2024)

*Heaven: Thinking Now about Forever* (Christian Publications; 2002)

*Insight from a Blind Man: A 1st Person Account of the Healing of the Man Born Blind. Me* (self-published; 2024)

*Living for Jesus in an Un-Christian World: A Study of the Epistle of Jude* (self-published; 2015)

*The Other Side of the Good News: Contemporary Challenges to Jesus' Teaching on Hell* (Christian Focus; 2003)

*Saved! Rescued from God, by God, and for God* (self-published, 2014)

*Stung! A Theophilus Hornby Mystery* (Energion; 2024)

*Ten Specific Steps You Can Take to Make Your Sermons and Preaching Better* (self-published; 2017)

*Thinking about Theology: A Collection of Theological Essays from the 2016 CIU Class* ("Theological Issues and Methods") (editor, self-published; 2016)

*The Top 10 Mistakes Students Make on Research Papers — And How to Avoid Them!* (self-published; 2014)

*Unlike Jesus: Let's Stop Unfriending the World* (Energion, 2019)

*Whatever Happened to Heresy?* (self-published; 2013)

*When Temptation Strikes: Gaining Victory Over Sin* (CLC Publications; 2008)

www.ingramcontent.com/pod-product-compliance
Lightning Source LLC
LaVergne TN
LVHW041207080426
835508LV00008B/833